Dreaming America:
Voices of Undocumented Youth
in Maximum-Security Detention

DREAMING AMERICA

Seth Michelson, Editor
Preface by Jimmy Santiago Baca

VOICES OF UNDOCUMENTED YOUTH
IN MAXIMUM-SECURITY DETENTION

SETTLEMENT HOUSE

Library of Congress
Control Number
2017935133
Michelson, Seth (editor)
Dreaming America: voices of undocumented
youth in maximum-security detention
ISBN: 978-0-9859468-9-0

First edition

Manufactured in the United States of America
Cover design by Ellen Hamilton
Type setting and composition by Sarah Fannon

SETTLEMENT HOUSE

www.settlementhouse.us
PO Box 12004
Silver Spring, MD 20908

ACKNOWLEDGMENTS

Seth Michelson's most recent book of poetry is *Swimming Through Fire* (Press 53, 2017). He teaches the poetry of the Americas at Washington and Lee University.

Jimmy Santiago Baca's latest book is *Singing at the Gates*, by Grove Press.

Cristina Casado is a Program Manager with the Office for Refugee Resettlement / Division of Children.

Support for the publication of this book was provided by the Class of 1956 Provost's Faculty Development Endowment at Washington and Lee University.

TABLE OF CONTENTS

Introduction—Seth Michelson, viii
Preface by Jimmy Santiago Baca, xvii

Dreaming

INTRODUCTION

Thank you for opening this book. It is a greeting and a lifeline, both of which depend upon you. That is, the following texts come to you directly from incarcerated teens living in isolation cells in one of two maximum-security detention centers for undocumented, unaccompanied youth in the United States. And from their solitude, they are reaching out to you.

By definition incarceration is isolating and aggrieving for the detainee, and this is certainly true of the lived experience of the teen authors herein. It bears immediate mention, too, that the detention center holding them is staffed by many good people, who strive daily to help the children. Nevertheless, incarceration wears on the mind and body.

To try to help the teens to cope with that wear, two years ago I offered to conduct poetry workshops with them in the facility. I'd found previous work in a men's maximum-security prison in New York to be deeply fulfilling for its participants, including me, and I'd hoped to build on that experience.

Simultaneously, I knew, too, that this work would be very different. First and foremost, I would be working this time with children. I also knew that they'd be coming to our workshop from life in isolation cells. Moreover, they were incarcerated in a new country, with unknown customs, a foreign language, unfamiliar foods, and a seemingly inscrutable system of jurisprudence. How could their experience be anything but traumatic?

As you'll soon see via their writing, it certainly is traumatic. Consequently, as you read their work, you might find yourself rethinking immigration policy and policing in the U.S. You might wonder, for example, how we as a democratic nation might best practice hospitality.

You might reasonably ask if incarceration is the best response to migration. And if so, should we consider the age of the the migrant? Should we concern ourselves with whether she migrated with family or alone? In other words, is it ethically tenable to incarcerate an unaccompanied child?

More theoretically, you might be inspired by this book to reflect on incarceration itself. You might reckon the conditions of captivity dictated by our legislature in our names as U.S. residents and citizens, and reconsider whether it is something to support or reform. For it is indisputable that the carceral system sows violence in its detainees' lives.

That violence is evident in multiple reports from the Immigration and Customs Enforcement (ICE) Office of Detention Oversight, the Department of Homeland Security (DHS), and many reputable news sources like The Pew Research Center, *The New York Times*, and *The Guardian*. From such sources, we know, for example, that more than three dozen adult detainees have died in ICE custody since May 2012, with many of those deaths attributed to suicide. The rate of self-injury among detainees is even higher, though precise figures are difficult to determine, particularly due to complexities and differences in identifying and reporting it.

What I can say with certainty is that self-harm and suicide are full-fledged crises among the child detainees with whom I worked to create this book. Sadly, too, this is perhaps unsurprising. Here are children who were born into extreme violence and poverty in some of the most dangerous places on Earth. On top of that, many were orphaned at a young age, leaving them to fend for themselves on uncommonly cruel streets. In the process they abandoned schooling, and so they average a second-grade education. To escape all of that violence and hopelessness, they fled north.

Dreaming America, they set out courageously on extraordinarily dangerous and lonely transnational journeys to try to transform their lives, and that was merely to arrive at our southern border. Once there, they still had to cross a perilous threshold that has claimed the lives of more than 6,000 migrants since 2000, according to the U.S. Border Patrol.

Only after surviving their grueling transcontinental trek and then the treacherous border crossing did they finally stand on U.S. soil, where most of them were thereupon swept up summarily by U.S. Border Patrol and ICE agents, often after little more than the briefest glimpse of our gorgeous country.

Consequently, most of the authors in this book have known little of the U.S. but its carceral system. In other words they know us only at our most rigid and punishing. Nevertheless, their hope springs eternal. Thus like all teens, these children carry detailed dreams of fabulous futures. They aspire to become chefs, politicians, mechanics, teachers, lawyers, rappers, and more. They want to be your friends, colleagues, neighbors, teammates, and employees. They also often want to become dutiful and proud U.S. citizens. But, for now, they languish in isolation cells in a maximum-security detention center. Is their penchant for self-harm and suicide really all that surprising?

Fortunately most undocumented, unaccompanied children are not detained so restrictively. In fact, maximum-security child detainees comprise less than one percent of the 59,692 unaccompanied minors that were apprehended along the southern border of the U.S. in 2016, for example. The vast majority of those children are placed in what amount to group homes, from which they integrate into and enrich local schools and communities, all while awaiting the court date on their Notice to Appear (NTA), when their case will be heard in immigration court and their residency status determined.

However, a small fraction of child detainees do face maximum-security detention, most often due to their personal histories, which might cause them to be categorized as posing a threat to themselves and/or others. This is often gang- and/or cartel-related, and it is very serious indeed. Nevertheless, these incarcerated teens, like any child, and especially any child in need, require our tenderness, patience, attention, and compassion. They are children in our care, and we therefore have an intrinsic responsibility to nurture them.

Hence my hope to spend time with them through poetry workshops. Poetry can prove a powerful tool for both introspection and interpersonal connection, and those twin possibilities seemed important to cultivate in relation to the presumed agonies of life in isolation cells in a foreign land.

Thankfully Cristina Casado, the visionary Program Manager from the Office of Refugee Resettlement, Division of Children's Service, in the detention center liked my proposal. She brought it to the attention of her superiors, who liked it, too, and soon the children and I were huddled around small metal tables, talking about poetry and writing it with tiny, rubber pencils.

Perhaps most importantly, the children showed an immediate joy in our meetings. Each visit found us delightedly enjoying one another's company through poetry, with each workshop finishing with a flourish of applause and cheers for each participant as he'd read out his new piece of writing to the group.

With each visit I marveled, too, at the striking courage of each child's writing. Time and again they created stunning testaments to human endurance, writing with precocious clarity about grisly violence, brutal heartbreak, and severe deprivation.

As I'd repeatedly point out to them, too, they were in this way testifying to their valor and resilience. And this was as evident in their delicate excavations of the past as their inspiring intimations of their dreamed futures.

Moreover, their thrumming industry in the workshops extended beyond each cluster of children and me. For example, Ms. Casado often joined us, too, saying it deepened her connections with the children, much to their mutual benefit. Likewise the counselors and corrections officers often mentioned to me their appreciation of the impact of the workshops on the children, who clearly relished the chance to write, read, and share poetry.

I'd like to think it has helped them each to cope at least a little better with his or her respective admixture of trauma, melancholy, and suffering. For without question, they were testifying in writing to their struggle to save their own lives. Moreover, they recognized and celebrated this in one another's testimony, which has to count for something, both in terms of developing self-knowledge and understandings of community. After all, these are hardscrabble children learning to trace the intricacies of one another's hearts, and the intimacy of such labor seems psychosocially and existentially healing.

I should mention, too, the timbre of our reunions. We always reconnect with smiles and fist bumps, happy to be again in one another's company. I've in fact felt warmly welcomed by them from our first meeting, and I've since come to care deeply for each of them. I greatly admire and them for many reasons, not the least of which is their courage as evident in their uncanny ability to write with trust and focus despite the circumstances of our meeting and the aftershocks of their agonizing childhoods and migrations.

So I hope, when reading their writing, you'll

sense how special they are. These are bright, imaginative, and insightful children, and when given the chance, they can transform worlds. Already they are helping us to rethink our very understanding of democracy. Here are tired and poor children yearning to breathe free; how best ought we receive and treat them?

More pointedly, what ethos do we espouse, both domestically and geopolitically, by placing traumatized child refugees in isolation cells in a maximum-security detention center? What alternatives might we conceive?

As usual the children offer helpful answers. Page by page, they suggest an array of possibilities for reconfiguring how we live. They expose myths of belonging and the anti-democratic lies of purity. In other words, the sophistication of their writing involves its inventive demonstrations of the power of hybridity. It shows how each of us is many, how we're each always already crossing borders, and how we demonstrate our humanity most clearly in our ability to engage desperate strangers. It is *e pluribus unum* as much as *novus ordo seclorum*.

To further explore the power of plurality in our poetry workshops, I created a new course last Fall for undergraduates at my home institution, Washington and Lee University. I titled it "Poetry and the Politics of Immigration," and through the course I taught immigrant poetry in literary, legal, and historiographical contexts to undergraduate students on campus on Mondays and Wednesdays. On Fridays I then brought the undergraduates to the detention center for a poetry workshop with the incarcerated children, pairing each undergrad with a detainee in each pod for the duration of the semester.

Together we wrote and shared, and each partnership maintained a collaborative writing journal, with the undergraduate translating her partner's work.

Of note, many of the texts in this book in fact began in those partnerships. Importantly, too, those workshops allowed the incarcerated children to meet and befriend young people from the U.S. For as aforementioned, most of the incarcerated children knew little more of our nation than our carceral system, so this chance to spend time with peers from beyond the facility proved especially welcome. And before long, we'd become a lively, complex, and thriving community with interlaced concerns and experiences.

Such is the power of poetry. It can recalibrate a reader's consciousness just as adeptly as it can convoke communities. It can stimulate creative solutions to impasses, and it can generate new forms of thinking within and against established epistemologies. It can reveal the resilience of human beings, and it can ravish our hearts, as you'll soon come to know. It can unveil differences for us to celebrate and cherish, and it can reveal the porosity of borders as they simultaneously connect and separate us.

In other words, in reading this book, you are bringing into being yet more links between our disparate and disciplined bodies, which are always already in multidirectional motion, and that's a dazzling, if dizzying, truth.

So on behalf of the incarcerated children, I thank you. On behalf of their undergraduate partners, I thank you. On behalf of the great artists Jimmy Santiago Baca and Ricardo Dominguez, each of whom joined us for a day in the detention center with the children, I thank you. And on behalf of Cristina Casado, I thank you.

We of course must also thank the detention center for its gracious support of these many, different workshops. And a special thanks is due, too, to Washington and Lee University for its institutional generosity.

I am especially indebted to my colleagues in the Romance Languages Department, who offered nothing less than their immediate, emphatic, and unwavering support of my work in the facility, both with and without our undergraduates. Likewise, David Buarte in the School of Law and Kirk Luder in University Counseling offered invaluable expertise and guidance. And the university administration has proven equally supportive. In particular I must offer a public thank you to Provost Marc Conner, Associate Provost Elizabeth Knapp, Coordinator of Community Engagement and Service Learning Linda Cummings, Dean Suzanne Keen, and Leanne Shank, Jennifer Kirkland, and Jana Shearer from the Office of Legal Counsel.

These allies, among many others, leapt at the chance to help to connect many previously disjointed and despairing young people into a vibrant and supportive community of writers.

With a deep bow I must thank, too, my intrepid troupe of undergraduates from "Poetry and the Politics of Belonging." They are Philip Aiken, Danielle Amiot, Connor Chess, Katie Clemmons, Erin Ferber, Ashby Gatens, Lorena Hernandez Barcena, Olivia Howell, and Kathryn Riley. They not only formed transformative friendships with their partners in the detention center, but also wrote beautiful letters to them and to the federal judges soon to hear their immigration cases.

Of note, the undergraduates are as disappointed as I am that we cannot for legal reasons identify the child authors of the original writing herein as they'd hoped and requested. It goes without mention that those brave, incarcerated children merit our heartiest acknowledgement, gratitude, and appreciation. They have left behind family and friends to traverse countries via perilous pathways, only to find themselves locked in cubicles of concrete and steel in the Land of the Free, where I am acutely aware of the painful irony in my obligation to publish their writing anonymously. In other words, in the very moment of the re-presentation their lives in writing to the public as a hopeful striving towards their return to visibility, I am obligated to anonymize their writing, thereby reinscribing their erasure from the body politic by the (unjust) law. Nevertheless, you'll still note how they blaze with creativity and generosity, how they still have faith in the goodwill of strangers, how they still believe in you. Along those lines, should you wish to express your support to them, then please feel welcome to write to me at my university address. If and when appropriate, I would gladly share your words of encouragement with the children during our continued workshops.

Last but not least, we all must offer a heartfelt thank you to Settlement House for publishing this book. As sponsor of the annual Settlement House American Poetry Prize, which honors the work of first-generation American poets, the press will donate proceeds from sales of this book to a legal defense fund for the incarcerated children, who are not constitutionally guaranteed lawyers on account of their status under U.S. law.

Of special note, too, this is also to say that Settlement House's generosity is yours. With your purchase of this book, you have helped these child refugees to fight for their dream of America. Here's to their life, liberty, and pursuit happiness, not to mention yours. May you one day meet in peace and freedom.

Seth Michelson
Lexington, Virginia, May 2017

PREFACE by Jimmy Santiago Baca

Seth and I drove out to the facility holding Mexican Nationals and Central Americans. These facilities of detainment always bring up in me a dark grief: I don't need to know the details of their journeys north, I've seen enough documentaries to know they have endured what few Americans can even tolerate for a minute. Look into their eyes and see all the poetry of universe spinning like orbs of fire, comets streaking across the dark skies of this country. Why lock them up like they are animals, like they are aliens, like they are illegal human beings? I get so angry with our feather-hearted politicians who serve the rich and torture the poor, and do so without an iota on consciousness.

We got to the facility, were escorted into the gym where they all gathered. I noticed the walls displayed the flags of many of the countries where the kids were from. I was here to share with them some poetry but I knew in my heart they carried more poetry in the tip of their index finger than I could ever hope to have. They sat in chairs arranged in a half circle. Brown faces. Brown eyes. Brown dreams that had been laid on the tracks and run over a thousand times only to rise again and move north—half starved, preyed upon by bandits and marauding gangs, each with a story and each with a story of someone else worse then they were.

I want to plead with America to please be kind to them, treat them with respect, offer them opportunity, show a little compassion: they are kids, children like our own but unlike our own, they are witnesses to our cruelty, human beings craving understanding and connection to us. And my only connection was my poetry which I read and they then took their turns reading. Everyone of them took a piece of my heart and I willingly gave it to them. They knew what I meant by heart, they knew darkness and isolation and mockery and crowds jeering at them and stereotyping them, they knew and still they hoped and dreamed and loved. And still, with parents murdered by cartels and tyrants and dictators, homes burned to the ground by military mercenaries, sisters and brothers raped and beat to death and imprisoned, they knew the meaning of life, were the very center and burning orb of Democracy— they nurtured Democracy in their words and actions and laughter and tears.

From out here, a distance of thousands of miles, in the high desert prairie, I bow in reverence to your spirits, I bow and pray and send sweet tidings my fellow brothers and sisters, endure, endure.

May 2017, Albuquerque, New Mexico

America

Tiempos malos

Para mí es bastante difícil recordar mi pasado porque es bastante malo.

Bad Times

It's very difficult for me to remember my past because it's very bad.

ONE / *UNO*

The Border

a place the whole world goes
when we dream
and want to see our families happy
but they don't let us reach the border
because we're from other countries
and I ask myself why
if we're all human beings
if we're all the same
don't we have papers too
because we're all in the same world
have the same feelings
though our skin colors may differ
but that doesn't mean we're not the same
it means that in this country in my country
there are lots of racists
to be white, to be black
doesn't mean we are
unequal
we're equal
we have the same thoughts
the same goal
to walk for days across the desert
called to immigrate

La frontera

un lugar a que todo el mundo vamos
al tener un sueño
y ver a mi familia feliz
pero no nos dejan llegar a la frontera
por ser de otro país
y me pregunto por qué
si todos somos seres humanos
somos los mismos
no tenemos papeles
porque estamos en el mismo mundo
tenemos sentimientos iguales
el color de piel es diferente
pero eso no quiere decir que no somos iguales
es que en este país en mi país
hay mucha gente racista
el ser blanco, el ser negro
no quiere decir
que somos iguales
somos todos iguales
tenemos la misma mente
la misma meta
el caminar días por el desierto
al inmigrar nos agarra

From the Earth

From the earth grew a fruit
so delicious
I paused to wonder,
Who harvested this fruit?

De la tierra

De la tierra creció una fruta,
Tan rica,
Que me puse a pensar,
¿Quién cosechó esa fruta?

I Forget

Without reason to exist
I often forget that I am
real and this makes ache
the soul that I don't have
or that can't find me
as I wander
somewhere else.

Olvido

Sin razón de existir
siempre olvido que soy
real y ésto hace que
me duela el alma
que no tengo o que
ando por algún lado
y no me encuentra.

The Future

The future is tricky because you often think everything will work out, only to have a last-minute decision change your life, your way of being, and your will to keep going. So it's sometimes better to think of your present, not your future.

My past is behind me, a past I enjoyed, but a mistake changed my life. And now I find myself in this place, behind four walls, and when I look to the skies, I see a present filled with anguish, agony, rejection, and missteps. But I often tell myself, "Even if I could change my past, I wouldn't change a thing because I learned a lot from the mistakes."

The important thing is to keep going, even if you have to put on a fake smile, because no one knows, nor could they imagine, what has happened in our lives. No one asked to come into this world, and sometimes there's no choice but to follow a given path. A lot happens in life, most of it sad, an occasional happiness, and sometimes you have no choice but to play the clown and laugh on the outside, even though inside we feel less than failures.

El futuro

El futuro es difícil porque muchas veces tú piensas que todo saldrá bien pero al final una respuesta te puede cambiar tu vida, tu forma de ser y tu entusiasmo de seguir adelante. Por eso a veces es mejor pensar en tu presente y no en tu futuro.

Atrás queda mi pasado, un pasado que disfruté, pero un error cambió mi vida. Y ahora me encuentro en un lugar bajo cuatro paredes, y cuando miro al cielo veo un presente de angustias, dolor, rechazos y caídas. Pero muchas veces me digo a mi mismo: "Si pudiera cambiar mi pasado, no cambiaría nada porque gracias a los errores aprendí mucho".

Lo importante es seguir adelante aunque muchas veces andas con una sonrisa fingida, pero nadie sabe ni se imagina lo que pasa por nuestras vidas. Nadie pidió venir al mundo y a veces no queda de otra que seguir este rumbo. Son muchas cosas que van en seguida en la vida, muchas tristezas, pocas alegrías, y a veces no te queda otra que hacer de payaso y reir por afuera aunque estemos sintiéndonos menos que fracasos.

Prison or Freedom

I grab paper and pencil,
write what I feel
directly to the prisons of the world,
the tigers are dozing,
the walls have spoken,
my feelings express solitude
and the devil pays me
in violence.

Prisión o libertad

Agarro papel y lápiz,
escribo lo que siento
directo a las prisiones del mundo,
los tigres están tomando siestas,
paredes hablaron,
mis sentimientos expresan la soledad
y el diablo me paga
con lo violento.

Donald Trump

Writing this song
I show Donald Trump
That Latinos have heart
That I'm no thief
That I rep my country
My Honduran heart
And that you're a pig
Sorry if I offend you
But this comes from deep within
With my heart open wide
I tell you you're swine
You don't know what you're doing
It's your fault we're being booted
It's our jobs we're losing
Damn fool, why you hassling us
If we've done nothing to you
Damn punk, you're offending us
With all the smack you're talking
It's our reputation you're destroying
My children you're hurting
With all the idiocy you're spewing
Why are you doing it
Soon you'll regret it
Latinos will destroy you
You don't know who you're messing with
You'll be deported from the universe
For all the dumb things you're doing
With that I'll say goodbye
Ask only that God forgive you
For all that you're doing
I hope it's us you keep offending

Donald Trump

Escribiendo esta canción
Le demuestro a Donald Trump
Que los latinos somos de corazón
Yo no soy ningún ladrón
Represento mi nación
Hondureño de corazón
Tu eres un cabrón
Disculpa si te ofendo
Pero todo esto me sale desde adentro
Con mi corazón abierto
Te digo que eres un puerco
No sabes lo que estás haciendo
Por tu culpa nos están despidiendo
Nuestro trabajos estamos perdiendo
Pinche culero por qué con nosotros te estás
      metiendo
Si nosotros nada te estamos haciendo
Pinche basura nos estás ofendiendo
Con toda la basura que estás diciendo
Nuestra reputación nos estás destruyendo
A mis hijos estás influyendo
Con toda la babosería que estás diciendo
Por qué lo estás haciendo
Poco a poco te vas a ir arrepintiendo
Los latinos te van a ir destruyendo
No sabes con quién te estás metiendo
Del mundo irás saliendo
Por todas las estupideces que estás haciendo
Con esto me voy despidiendo
Sólo le pido a Dios que te perdone
Por lo que estás haciendo
Ojalá que nos sigas ofendiendo

Memories from My Past

It was a gorgeous day;
I woke in the morning.
I decided to travel in search
of a better life.
I left my house.
I took a bus and told
my relatives I'd be back
soon to see them. I arrived at
Honduras' border with Guatemala.
Some officials detained me.
They tell me, You can't leave
your country, and I said, Why not?
You're a minor You have to be
accompanied by an adult.
The officials got distracted
and I ran for it.
Then I hopped a train. After
I'd made it about 50 km,
they detained the train
and yelled at me "Stop, Stop" but I kept
running to where they couldn't see me.
Later I made it to a well-known
place and took a bus
and then I met my sister
in a bus station
and she told me, "We're going
to my husband's house. We live in
Mexico City."

Recuerdos de mi pasado

Era un día muy hermoso;
desperté en la mañana.
Decidí viajar en busca
de una vida mejor.
Salí de mi casa.
Tome un autobús y les dije
a mis familiares que pronto
volvería a verlos. Llegue a la
Frontera Honduras con Guatemala.
Me detuvieron unos oficiales.
Me dicen tú no puedes salir
de tu país y les dije ¿por qué?
Eres menor tienes que ir
acompañado con un adulto.
Se descuidaron los oficiales
y corrí así de aquel lado.
Luego agarré el tren. Como
a 50 km estaba de migración,
detuvieron el tren y me
decían — párate, párate — y seguí
corriendo así a donde no me vieron.
Luego llegué a un lugar muy
conocido y tome un autobús
y luego encontré a mi hermana
en la central de autobuses
y me dijo — vamos a casa
de mi esposo. Vivimos en la
ciudad de México.

Memory and Future

When I think of El Salvador I grow
sad at not being with my family.

When I think of my family I at times
feel sad, at times happy for
the good memories.

When I think of my future I think of
leaving this place. I'm curious to be
out, but also a little nervous because
I don't know life here.

For me rebirth would be a wonderful thing,
to not have committed what I did in my country,
where I'd wanted to become an artist.

Recuerdo y futuro

Cuando pienso en El Salvador me pongo
triste por no estar con mi familia.

Cuando pienso en mi familia a veces
siento triste, a veces feliz por algunos
recuerdos buenos.

Cuando pienso en mi futuro pienso en
salir de este lugar. Me siento curioso por estar
afuera pero también un poco nervioso porque
nunca he conocido aquí.

Para mí el renacer sería algo maravilloso,
para no cometer lo que hice en mi país
y quisiera haber sido un dibujante.

Hate

You enter, are
here speaking with me,
while others keep vigil
over their parents' deaths,
while you and I are talking
others are at war,
others are killing boys and girls,
others are crying, others laugh,
others suffer,
others dance, and still others shout,
and I mull
my life's frustrations.
If they wanted to write
what I know to be
happening, there wouldn't be
ink
or paper enough
to write
everything that could be seen.

El odio

Entras, tú estás
aquí hablando conmigo,
otros están velando
a los muertos de sus padres,
otros están en guerra en lo que
tú y yo estamos hablando,
otros están matando niños y niñas,
otros lloran, otros ríen,
otros agonizan,
otros bailan y otros gritan,
y yo repaso las
agravaciones de mi vida.
Si quisiera escribir
lo que sé que está
pasando, ni la tinta
ni el papel me bastaría
escribir en
todo lo que vea.

Poetry

Poetry is a form of explaining your feelings to yourself, someone else, or many others, a way of freeing yourself from the chains that tie you to harsh reality. Poetry is also a kind of description that defines who you are and who you will be in life.

La poesía

La poesía es una forma de explicar tus sentimientos a tí mismo, otra persona o muchas personas, una manera de liberarte de las cadenas que te atan a la dura realidad. También la poesía es un tipo de descripción que define quién eres y serás en la vida.

Dreaming

TWO / *DOS*

Crossing Borders

There are many things to go through
in the world, like when one
has a girlfriend, you go through
many things
first a talk and then you know each other
it's like when one has
a friend, one is always crossing
borders.

Like the tree when the apple
falls, it's a step
the tree takes.

Today I'm like a tree. When
chopped down, the tree has to leave
its roots, and it hurts, but soon
the roots grow a new tree.

Cruzar fronteras

Las cosas que pasan en el mundo
son muchas como cuando uno
tiene una novia, pasas por
muchas cosas
primero una plática después se conocen
es igual cuando uno conoce
a un amigo uno siempre cruza
fronteras.

Como el árbol cuando cae
la manzana, es un paso que
dé el árbol.

Hoy yo estoy como un árbol. Cuando
lo cortan, el árbol tiene que dejar
sus raíces, y le duele, pero pronto
las raíces crecen otro árbol.

Marriage

Yesterday in my cell
my pal asked, Man,
don't you want to marry life
forever? And I
answered, Why
marry life
if I can't divorce
death?

El casamiento

Ayer en mi celda me
dijo mi compañero, mira
¿quieres casarte con la vida
para siempre? Y yo le
contesté ¿para qué
casarme con la vida
si no puedo divorciarme
de la muerte?

Live at Peace with Your Past

Live at peace with your past.
Do the things that make you happy.
Enjoy each step. It's not as important
to arrive as to enjoy the journey.
Don't compare yourself to anyone, you're singular.
Change what you must,
though you can only change yourself.
It's you who's 100% of your happiness and
        no one else.
It's free to smile and it inspires life. Cry
if you must, but smile after.

All you have in life
are options.
You give in or fight
for what you want.
Don't wait for it to come to you,
go running in search of it.

Vive en paz con tu pasado

Vive en paz con tu pasado.
Haz las cosas que te hacen felíz.
Disfruta cada paso. No es tan importante
llegar como disfrutar el camino.
No te compares con nadie, eres único.
Cambia lo que tengas que cambiar,
pero sólo pueda cambiarte a ti mismo.
Eres tu el 100% de tu felicidad tú y nadie más.
Sonreir es gratis y da vida. Llora si tienes
que llorar y después sonríe.

Sólo tienen opciones
en la vida.
Te cedes o luchas
por lo que quieres.
No esperas que llegue,
corres a buscarlo.

Today

Today I want to tell you how I feel about you. I want to tell you so many things that I don't know how to say. I feel something immense that I can't resist. Everything I feel is only for you. I love you above all else, even if you doubt it. I want to tell you all of this personally, but you won't give me the chance to express my love to you. I only want the chance to explain to you what I feel and to never stop loving you, and if you tell me that you don't feel anything for me, then I'll stop bothering you. My queen, I only want the chance to express to you the enormity of my love. It's so very difficult for me to have you so close but to be unable to hug you or kiss you. I want you to know that my love knows no limits. You're just so beautiful, more beautiful than a rose. You're the most precious woman in the world. Every second that you're somewhere I'd like to be drives me crazy. I know it's hard to explain, so maybe it's best we go somewhere beyond this world without a path. I only want to be with you. It's you who drives my life. It's you who are my happiness. You're everything I've ever wanted. The only thing I want you to tell me now is if you want me to surrender my love and my heart to you.

Hoy

Hoy quiero decirte lo que yo siento por tí. Quiero decirte tantas cosas que no sé cómo decir. Siento algo imenso que no puede resistir. Todas las cosas que siento sólo son por tí. Te amo por encima de todo aunque lo dudes. Quiero decirte todo esto personal pero tú no me das la oportunidad de expresarte mi amor. Yo sólo quiero una oportunidad para explicarte lo que yo siento y nunca dejar de amarte, y si me dices que no sientes nada por mí voy a dejar de molestarte. Mi vida, sólo quiero un chance para demostrarte mi amor en grande. Es que ésto es muy difícil para mí tenerte tan cerca y no poder abrazarte o besarte. Quiero que sepas que mi amor no tiene limitación. Es que eres tan hermosa, más que una rosa. Eres la mujer más preciosa del mundo. Por tí me vuelvo loco cada segundo que tú eres en un lugar en el que yo quisiera estar. Sé que es muy difícil de explicar, así que mejor vámonos a un lugar fuera de este mundo sin rumbo. Sólo quiero estar contigo. Eres tú la persona que conduce mi vida. Eres tú mi alegría. Eres todo lo que siempre quería. Ahora sólo quiero que me digas si quieres que te entregue mi amor y mi corazón.

When I Saw You

When I saw you a while back
I asked my God
to send me someone
like you. Of all
the Roses you're the
most beautiful, though the
word *beautiful* falls
short of how
gorgeous and precious you are.
Drugs were my
worst therapist. They never
cured me. I want only
to go to a desert
where you and I'd be
alone together.

Cuando yo te vi

Cuando yo te vi hace
tiempo le pedí a mi Dios
que me mandara algo
como vos. De todas
las Rosas eres la
más hermosa aun la
palabra hermosa se
queda corta para lo
bella y preciosa que eres
La droga fue mi
peor psicólogo. Nunca me han
curado. Sólo quiero
ir a un desierto
donde tú y yo estemos
solos.

Hi Love

Hi love, I looked for you
but couldn't find you,
and now I have.
Hello my hope,
where have you been?
Hello peace,
where were you in my mind?
I couldn't find you.
Hello contempt,
where were you?
You've always been here.
Hello hatred,
where were you?
I've gone seconds without seeing you.
Bitterness,
thank you for feeding me
and giving me life.
Without you I don't know what
I'd be, I'd be someone
without emotions, without reason
to exist or reason to live.

Hola amor

Hola amor te busqué
y no te encontraba,
pero ahora te encontré
Hola esperanza mía,
¿dónde te habías ido?
Hola paz,
¿dónde estabas en mi mente?
No te encontraba.
Hola desprecio,
¿dónde estabas tú?
Siempre estuviste aquí.
Hola odio,
¿dónde estabas?
Tenía segundos de no verte.
Rencor,
gracias por alimentarme
y darme vida.
Sin tú no sé qué
sería yo, sería alguien
sin emociones, sin razón
para existir y sin razón de vivir.

To My Mother

you're that person who
makes my life better,
whenever I see you,
you make my heart happy

your lips are red
as an apple
that sweetens me
each morning

your eyes shine
like super giant
diamonds

you're the best thing
that's ever happened to me
I love you mom.

A mi madre

tu eres esa persona que
haces mi vida mejor,
siempre que te veo,
me alegras el corazón

tus labios son rojos
como una manzana
que me endulza
todas las mañanas

tus ojos son brillantes
como unos diamantes
súper gigantes

tu eres lo mejor
que me ha pasado
te amo mamá.

Blows in Life

There are such brutal blows in life, like when you lose someone, a parent, that's the worst thing that can happen, or you lose a good friend to the streets and he was like a brother, or like when your dad doesn't love you and you see everyone else and recognize what they have: their parents love them, it makes you feel hideous, it's something no one wants in his heart, you're sad, you feel alone and cry, what more can I say?

Los golpes en la vida

Hay golpes en la vida tan fuertes como cuando pierdes a alguien, a un padre, eso es lo peor que te puede pasar, o pierdes un buen amigo tuyo por la calle y fue casi un hermano, o como cuando tu padre no te quiere y miras a los demás y te das cuenta de lo que tienen: sus padres los quieren, te hacen sentir feo, es algo en el corazón que a uno no le gusta, estás triste, te sientes solo y lloras, ¿qué más te puedo decir?

Loneliness

There are such brutal blows in life
when someone wanders lost
through the streets and can't find
a way out and sees people
that humiliate him and reject him
and then comes the sadness and
loneliness.

La soledad

*Hay golpes en la vida tan fuertes
cuando una persona anda perdida
en las calles y no encuentra
cómo salir y ve a las personas
que la humillan y la rechazan
y entonces viene la tristeza y la
soledad.*

The Tear

A tear doesn't mean
you're sad
but rather that you feel bad
because sadness and feeling bad
are different.
Bad is when you can't go on
but when you're sad,
one word can make you
better. See?
Don't get confused.

La lágrima

Una lágrima no se significa
que estás triste
sino que estás mal
porque tristeza y sentirse mal
es diferente.
Mal es que ya no puede continuar
y cuando estás triste,
una palabra te vuelve a hacer
sentir bien. ¿Ves?
No te confundas.

Dreaming

THREE / *TRES*

Border Crossings

When you have problems in your life
and you don't know what you're doing, all the ideas
in your head, some good,
some bad, confuse you,
and they take you to a place where
your thoughts change daily and you
feel very depressed about the
situation you find yourself in
without knowing what to do, trying to
choose between all the thoughts
you have, whether to move on
or stay stuck in your pain and
confusion. I can only tell you
God has a solution for everything.
If you never try, you'll never know.
Because if God wants to act, no one can
stop him.

Cruzamientos de fronteras

Cuando tienes problemas en tu vida
y no sabes qué haces, tantas ideas
en tu cabeza, unas buenas,
otras malas, las cuales te confunden
y te llevan a un mundo donde el
pensar se convierte a diario y te
sientes muy deprimido por la
situación en que te encuentras
sin saber qué hacer, tratar de
escoger entre tantas ideas que
tienes, si seguir o quedarte
estacionado con tu dolor y tu
confusión. Sólo puedo decirte
Dios para todo tiene una solución.
Si nunca lo intentas, jamás lo sabrás.
Porque si Dios quiere actuar, nadie puede
impedirlo.

I don't want to do anything . . .

I'd have liked to see my mom,
But she wasn't good to me.
She never told me I love you,
Called me a street kid.
I'd always wanted her to love me,
I want you to tell me I'm yours, son,
That you love me.
But it won't happen because she's dead.
And I don't feel anything,
Her life doesn't matter to me. . .

In my room I always cry.
My crying in my room is like heavy rain.
At night I always ask God
To give me a mother that loves me.

"Our Father, Jesus of Nazareth!
Considering your goodness
And your love for me,
A cry of gratitude escapes my lips,
Telling you,
Dear Jesus, I love you!
For our love, you descended to Earth
And you suffered bitter pain,
Dying nailed to a cross,
For our love, you gave us the sacrament
Of our alters to feast on,
For our love,
You appeared in that blessed image,
Crowned with thorns,
With sad eyes and a sorrowing face,

continue, p. 70

No quiero hacer nada . . .

Quisiera ver a mi mamá,
Pero no era buena conmigo.
Nunca me dijo te quiero,
Que yo era de la calle.
Siempre quisiera que me quiera.
Quiero que me digas soy tuyo, hijo,
Que tú me amas,
Pero no porque está muerta.
Pero yo me siento nada,
No me importa la vida de ella. . .

Siempre en mi cuarto me pongo a llorar.
El ver mucha lluvia es como lloro en mi cuarto.
Siempre estoy en la noche pidiéndole a Dios
Que me diera una madre que sí me quiera.

> "¡Padre nuestro Jesús Nazareno!
> Al considerar vuestra bondad
> Y vuestro amor para mí,
> Un grito de gratitud sale de mis labios,
> Diciéndoos
> ¡Jesus mio, os amo!
> Por nuestro amor bajasteis a la tierra
> Y sufristeis dolores acerbisimos,
> Muriendo clavado en una cruz,
> Por nuestro amor os disteis como manjar
> En el sacramento de nuestros altares,
> Por nuestro amor
> Os manifestáis en esa imagen bendita,
> Coronado de espinas,
> Con los ojos lánguidos y el rostro dolorido,

continuar, p. 71

The symbol of your suffering.
Thank you, God!
And to repay so many favors
I beg you the grace
To always uphold your holy law
And die in your love.
Amen."

I ask this of you, God,
So that you'll give me a mother.

Símbolo de vuestro sufrimiento.
¡Gracias, Señor!
Y para corresponder a tantos favores
Os pido la gracia
De cumplir siempre vuestra ley santa
Y de morir en vuestro amor
Amen."

Porque lo pido Dios,
Pa'que me de una madre.

The Lonely Angel

Suddenly I stop flying,
look around and see things
that break my heart,
I see beautiful things.
Beautiful, but I can't touch them.

I see evil and can't quit it.
It's like my shadow that follows me,
but saddest of all is the lonely angel.
Only because he can't fly.

Because I trusted someone
and as always betrayed him.
Because he trusted someone and was betrayed,
I pity the lonely angel.

I look in the mirror
and see I'm the lonely angel
and am stunned that I pity myself.

El ángel solitario

De repente dejo de volar,
veo alrededor y miro cosas
que me parten el corazón,
veo cosas bellas.
Bellas, pero no puedo tocarlas.

Veo maldad y no puedo dejarme de ella.
Es como mi sombra que me persigue,
pero lo más triste es el ángel solitario.
Sólo porque no puede volar.

Porque confío en alguien
y como siempre, lo traicioné.
Porque confió en alguien que lo traicionó,
me compadezco con el ángel solitario.

Pero me miro en el espejo
y veo que el ángel solitario soy
y me sorprende con compadecerme de mí mismo.

How to Live

One doesn't know nor is he born knowing how to live life, instead he's born to learn to live it. To be born, to reproduce, and finally to die. Without death there's no life, without life there's no death, and without either there's just the emptiness accompanied and captured by the spirit of solitude, whose pressure attacks you like a wild beast waiting to strike at the opportune moment.

Cómo vivir

Uno no sabe ni nace sabiendo cómo vivir la vida, sino que nace para aprender a vivirla. Nacer, reproducir y por último morir. Sin la muerte no hay vida, sin la vida no hay muerte y sin ninguna es el vacío acompañado y apañado con las garras de la soledad donde la presión te ataca como una fiera esperando atacar en el momento oportuno.

If a man could . . .

cry without shame, ask forgiveness,
without our pride
or ego getting hurt, or if you could say
to yourself I forgive you because
you've behaved badly, but
to yourself, because it's easy
to forgive people of importance to you,
the tricky thing is to forgive
yourself, to say to yourself I forgive you, because
one sees the defects of others,
but to see your own and forgive them
is very hard, but try, friends,
it will be easy in the end.

Si el hombre pudiera . . .

llorar sin pena, pedir perdón,
sin que nuestro orgullo
o el ego se dañaría, o si pudieras decir
a tí mismo te perdono porque
te has portado muy mal pero
contigo mismo, porque es fácil
perdonar personas que te importan
pero el problema es perdonarse
a sí mismo, decirte te perdono, porque
uno mira los defectos de los demás,
pero mirarse sus defectos y perdonarlos
es muy difícil, pero traten compañeros
que se les hará fácil al final.

The Future

The future is something new
that comes bit by bit.

The bad, the mistakes
and pain, remain behind.

The important thing is to keep
going in life and see
the best of the world,
nature.

It's best to keep
moving even though
your problems
will follow you.

El futuro

El futuro es algo nuevo
que pasa poco a poco.

Atrás queda lo malo,
los errores y dolores.

Lo importante es seguir
con la vida y ver
lo mejor del mundo,
la naturaleza.

Adelante hay que
seguir aunque
los problemas
te empiezan a perseguir.

To Have a Dream

I dream of being the president of my country
I dream of discovering a world where nothing would
    matter more than what you carry within

Tener un sueño

Sueño con ser el presidente de mi país
Sueño con descubrir un mundo donde no importe
nada más que sólo lo que llevas dentro de ti

I Want to Support †

I want to support the
poor and end
hunger. I'd like to give
a great place to live
to those
without one, and also
to the animals.

† *The poem was written above a drawing of a rainbow, a tree,
and the poet's family, including his wife, son, and him.*

Quiero apoyar †

*Yo quiero apoyar a los
pobres y acabar con el
hambre. Los que no
tienen donde vivir
quisiera darles un lugar
para desear, y también
a los animales.*

*† El poema fue escrito arriba de un dibujo de un arcoiris, un
árbol y la familia del poeta, incluso su esposa, un hijo y él.*

After I Fled

After I fled my country, everything became an adventure because I'd left the world I'd been living in; it doesn't feel good to know that everyone is afraid of you. It turns you into a monster, which is what they think of people like me. They can't imagine that everything I did, I did out of fear. Fear they'd hurt my family: but all of that is done.

Después de haber salido

Después de haber salido huyendo de mi país, todo se convirtió en una aventura porque pude salir del mundo en que estaba viviendo; no siente bien saber que todas las personas te tienen miedo. Eso te convierte en un monstruo. Eso es lo que piensan las personas de mí. No se imaginan que todo lo que hice, lo hice por miedo. Miedo a que lastimaran a mi familia: pero todo eso se terminó.

Rebirth

I'd begin the rebirth with myself. Because one day I thought that I could change the world, but I was wrong. And I thought I could change my country, but I was wrong then, too. And I thought that I could change my family, but I was very wrong there. And so I think about changing myself. Because if I were to change myself first, then I'd also be changing my family and country, and probably the world. Still we'll sometimes think we need to change what's around us first. But that's not right. We need to change ourselves. We might see the world one way, while reality is another. But one day, my day to be reborn will come, and I'll be able to do many things to help not only myself and my family, but also everyone in need throughout the world.

Renacimiento

Empezara mi renacimiento con yo mismo. Porque un día pensé que podía cambiar el mundo pero estaba equivocado. Y pensé que podía cambiar mi país pero también estaba equivocado. Y pensé que podía cambiar mi familia y también estaba muy equivocado. Y entonces pienso en cambiar a yo mismo. Porque si fuera cambiando yo mismo primero, también hubiera cambiado mi familia y también mi país y probablemente mi mundo. Pero a veces pensamos que primero tenemos que cambiar nuestro alrededor. Pero no es así primero. Tenemos que cambiar a nosotros mismo. Vemos al mundo como nosotros somos a veces pero la realidad es otra. Pero algún día llegara mi día apropiado para tomar mi renacimiento y así podré hacer muchas cosas que no sólo ayuden a mí mismo y a mi familia, sí ayuden a todo el mundo que lo necesita.

Dreaming

FOUR / *CUATRO*

Crossing Borders

There are borders in life.
It's very hard to learn English,
But I'm trying.
I try because
I want to be someone in life,
I want to live here,
In the United States.
I want break through this border to help my family,
To teach them what I've learned,
Like my English.
I can help to change our lives,
Teach them what life is like in another country.
These borders are hard to cross
With their fears, furies, frustrations.
But I keep fighting to learn.
Although borders are hard
To traverse
I'll one day make it across and improve my life.

Cruzar fronteras

Hay fronteras en la vida,
Para aprender inglés es algo difícil,
Para mí lo intento.
Lo prueba porque
Quiero ser alguien en la vida,
Para vivir aquí,
En los Estados Unidos.
Romper esa frontera para ayudar a mi familia,
Enseñarles lo que he aprendido,
Como el inglés.
Puedo ayudar a cambiar nuestras vidas,
Enseñarles como son las vidas en otro país.
Estas fronteras son difíciles de cruzar
Con nervios, enojos, frustraciones.
Pero sigo con la lucha de aprender.
Aunque las fronteras son difíciles
De superar
Algún día lo cruzo y mejoraré la vida.

The Good Times

The good times are the
most beautiful things life offers
and that's why we must keep
struggling because we'll always have
good times and it's the boost
life gives us so that we'll fight
for our goals and thoughts
that we have in life,
goals and thoughts
that our family
and community will feel proud
of us because if someday
they feel disconnected from our
lives, well that's the moment
for them to know
we can achieve
anything we want, let's get
going and never stop.

Los tiempos buenos

Los tiempos buenos son los
más bonitos que la vida nos da
y por eso hay que echarle ganas
a la vida porque siempre tendremos
tiempos buenos y es un empujón que
la vida nos da para que luchemos
con nuestra metas y pensamientos
que tenemos en nuestra vida
metas y pensamientos que
tengamos para que nuestra familia
y la sociedad se sientan orgullosas
de nosotros porque si algún día
se sintieron desconectadas de nuestra
vida pues allí es el momento
para que sepan que también
nosotros podemos cumplir
todo lo que queremos échemelo para
delante no nos detengamos nunca.

Being Here

I'm thankful for:
the future when I might be able to change my life
        for the better,
I hope to stay here so I can change my life.
Learn English and study and better myself.
Make good friends.

Estar aquí

Estoy agradecido por:
el futuro porque quizás puedo cambiar mi vida
        a otra mejor,
espero quedarme aquí para cambiar mi vida.
Poder aprender inglés y estudiar y mejorar.
Encontrar amigos buenos.

My Dog Spay

is small,
is white and brown,
gets angry with other people.
But with my family, he's happy.

With me he's happy, I played
with him when he was young.
I'd run around the house
and he'd follow.
When he couldn't catch me,
he'd start to cry.
Whenever I'd go to leave,
he'd throw himself on me,
the dude would bite me
and lock me down.
To make him release me,
I'd stroke him
till the dude and I came apart.

Being without him now
makes me feel like
I have nothing
in my life.

And when we see each other
he's going to be so happy
he'll start
jumping like crazy.

Mi perro Spay

es pequeño,
es blanco con café,
es muy enojado con otras personas.
Con mi familia es muy alegre.

Conmigo es alegre, jugaba
con él cuando era pequeño.
Yo corría alrededor de la casa
y el me seguía.
Cuando no me alcanzaba,
se ponía a llorar.
Cuando yo iba,
él se me tiraba encima
y me mordía el choy
y se quedaba enllavado en mi choy.
Cuando lo hacía que se soltaba,
me ponía a acariciarlo
para que se soltara del choy

Ahora estar sin él
me hace sentir como
que nunca lo haya comprado
en mi vida.

Y cuando nos veamos
se va a alegrar mucho
que se va a poner a
saltar como loco.

Memories

I still remember
that special time
when my family would laugh
about whatever happened,
everything was so happy.

Those Sundays at church
and then lunch at home.

The days at the ranch on the beach,
everyone having fun with *carne asada*,
beers, bonfires, running on the
beach with a cigar
in hand, thinking
of the future.

Time passes,
things change,
but soon everything
will be like it was
before.

Recuerdos

Todavía recuerdo
ese momento tan especial
donde mi familia reía
por las cosas que pasaban,
todo era tan feliz.

Esos domingos en la iglesia
y luego el almuerzo en la casa.

Los días en el rancho de la playa
todos divirtiéndose con carne asada,
cervezas, fogatas, correr en la
playa con un cigarro
en la mano, pensando
en el futuro.

El tiempo pasa,
las cosas cambian,
pero pronto todo
será igual que
antes.

Untitled

I tried to kill myself 6 times without succeeding, but I know that day or night the moment will have to come when from a slip I'll lose my life and that's why I don't long to become a poet or scientist or pastor or president or to be someone prestigious because what's the point of knowing so much if with a blow to the head I'd forget everything unable even to remember my name.

Sin título

Me he intentado suicidar 6 veces pero ninguna con éxito, pero sé que tarde o noche tendrá que llegar el momento que de un trompezón se me vaya la vida por eso no anhelo ser un poeta o un científico o un pastor o un presidente o ser alguien prestigiado porque de qué me sirve saber tanto si con un golpe en la cabeza olvidaría todo ni tan siquiera me acordaría de mi nombre.

To Get Out One Day

To get out one day and
live a beautiful
life going forward.

To be outside and
form a new life
I want to be
with my family.

I want to go with my family,
we'll go to the beach
and my heart will be there
with my family.

In life to go
and arrive
at a place I want
to arrive at, and where I know
I'll achieve it and
triumph in life.

Un día salir

Un día salir y
vivir una vida
hermosa por seguir.

Afuera estar y
una vida nueva
formar con mi familia
quiero estar.

Quiero ir con mi familia,
podemos ir a la playa
y con mi familia mi
corazón estará allá.

En la vida ir
y llegar a un
lugar donde quiero
llegar y yo sé que lo
voy a lograr y en la
vida triunfar.

I have a dream . . .

to fill the emptiness that's in me.
I'd like to be surrounded by friends,
people that are important to me and care for me,
even though I don't care what happens with my life.

There's only one thing that's important to me.
It's that my family be well
and happy,
even though I probably won't be.

I don't know what will happen with my life.
But I don't worry about that.
My life has been a disaster
and I don't think that will change.

The only thing I hope for
is that you all are happy
and follow your dreams.

Yo tengo un sueño . . .

Llenar el vacío que hay en mí.
Me gustaría estar rodeado de amigos,
personas que me importen y se preocupen por mi,
aunque no me importa lo que pasó con mi vida.

Sólo hay una cosa que me importa.
Es que mi familia se encuentre bien
y sea feliz,
aunque creo que tal vez yo no lo será.

No sé qué pasará con mi vida.
Pero no me preocupo por eso.
Mi vida ha sido un desastre
y no creo que eso cambiaré.

Lo único que espero
es que todos ustedes sean feliz
y sigan con sus sueños.

The Future

The future is for forgetting
the past and the suffering

The mistakes stay behind

The important thing is that still
there is life

Ahead is our destiny,
our life

El futuro

El futuro es olvidar
el pasado y el sufrimiento

Atrás quedaron los errores

Lo importante es que todavía
hay vida

Adelante es nuestro destino,
nuestra vida

REFLECTION by Cristina Casado

Unaccompanied Children are placed under the Office for Refugee Resettlement (ORR)/ Division of Children Services (DCS) after being apprehended by the Department of Homeland Security (DHS) for having no lawful immigration status in the United States, not having attained 18 years of age, and having no parent or legal guardian in the United States available to provide care and physical custody. Unaccompanied Children placed in the most restrictive setting, as the one where these poetry workshops took place, represent less than one percent of the 59,170 children referred to the ORR/DCS in 2016.

Most Unaccompanied Children placed in a secure setting have a behavioral or criminal history, accompanied by significant abuse, trauma, and neglect in their home countries. Working with these children in a secure environment is a difficult but extremely rewarding experience. Washington and Lee University students worked closely and individually with them for more than three months, helping them to express themselves positively through poetry. As a result, they were able to "tell their stories" of immigration, recounting a traumatic journey north as they escaped poverty and violence. Through their narratives, they transparently and openheartedly expressed their feelings of isolation, anxiety over an uncertain present, and hopes for a better life and a second chance. Week after week, the children polished their writing skills and presented beautiful renditions such as this:

De la tierra creció una fruta,	From the earth grew a fruit
Tan rica,	so delicious
Que me puse a pensar,	I paused to wonder,
¿Quién cosechó esa fruta?	Who harvested this fruit?

The lasting benefits and legacy of this collaboration have no boundaries, particularly during these politically tumultuous times when walls are built to isolate the most vulnerable of populations: children. It is through programs as these that allow for Unaccomanied Children's voices to be heard, where borders are erased momentarily, where healing can begin, and where the children are allowed to belong and be free. These children have been inspired to continue to express themselves long after the program concluded and their stories told.

Staunton, Virginia, April 2017

SETTLEMENT HOUSE POETRY

The Carnival, The Life—David Allan Evans
*Bloodroot—Catherine Jagoe
*Dreaming America: Voices of Undocumented Youth in
Maximum-Security Detention*—Edited by Seth Michelson
South Pole / Polo Sur—Maria Teresa Ogliastri (translated
by Yvette Neisser Moreno and Partricia Bejarano Fisher)
* Flowering Fires / Fuegos Florales—Alicia Partnoy
(translated by Gail Wronsky)
King Philip's War—Sheppard Ranbom
The Lunatic in the Trees—Dennis Sampson
Within the Shadow of a Man—Dennis Sampson
As Sunrise Becomes the World: A Trilogy—Louie Skipper
It Was the Orange Persimmon of the Sun—Louie Skipper
The Work Ethic of the Common Fly—Louie Skipper
The Unattended Harp—Peter Waldor
** Who Touches Everything—Peter Waldor
The Importance of Being Zimmer—Paul Zimmer

* Settlement House American Poetry Prize **National
Jewish Book Award, 2013

*Settlement House Books, Inc., is an independent, non-profit
501(c)(3) book publisher. Founded in 2007, we take our name
from the settlement houses of the late 19th, 20th and current cen-
turies that provided community—and continue to do so—through
their social and cultural support of and service to urban poor
and immigrant populations. In that spirit, we think of ourselves
as a home for some of the voices of poetry deserving of great-
er readership now and in the future. www.settlementhouse.us*